Positive Thinking

Susan Quilliam

LONDON, NEW YORK, MUNICH,
MELBOURNE, DELHI

Editor Elizabeth Watson
Designer Vicky Read
Production Editor Ben Marcus
Production Controller Anna Wilson
Executive Managing Editor Adèle Hayward
Art Director Peter Luff
Category Publisher Stephanie Jackson

Produced for Dorling Kindersley by

studio cactus ☉

13 SOUTHGATE STREET WINCHESTER HAMPSHIRE SO23 9DZ

Designer Dawn Terrey
Editor Sue Gordon
Managing Editor Mic Cady

First published in Great Britain in 2003
This edition published in Great Britain in 2008
by Dorling Kindersley Limited, 80 Strand
London WC2R 0RL

A Penguin Company

4 6 8 10 9 7 5 3

Copyright © 2003
Dorling Kindersley Limited
Text copyright © 2003 Susan Quilliam

A CIP catalogue record for this book is available
from the British Library

ISBN: 987-1-4053-2836-4

Reproduced by Colourscan, Singapore
Printed and bound in China by WKT

See our complete catalogue at

www.dk.com

Contents

3

Introduction

*I*n today's challenging world it is vital to
have energy, enthusiasm, and optimism
in all areas of your life. Positive Thinking
shows you how to transform your approach
to living, so you can feel good about yourself,
create worthwhile relationships, and perform
successfully. Having helped you identify areas
of negativity in your life, the book shows you
how to rethink negative beliefs, optimize
self-esteem, and learn new mental and
emotional strategies for affirmative, effective
thinking. Self-assessment exercises enable you
to evaluate your positivity. The book then helps
you apply these fundamental lessons to your
life – in the workplace, in love, for health, at
play, and in friendship. A solid foundation of
positivity will help you get the best from life.

Understanding Positive Thinking

Thinking positively helps you get the best out of life. The first step in making your life more positive is to become aware of your feelings, thoughts, and beliefs.

Grasping the Key Concepts

To understand positive thinking, begin with an overview of its benefits and how it works. At work or play, with friends or family, positive people are happier and more successful than those with a negative approach. Put simply, positivity works.

FOCUS POINT

● Positive people achieve more, stay healthier, and have better relationships than negative thinkers.

WHAT IS POSITIVE THINKING?

Positive thinking is about more than the thoughts that you have. It is an entire approach to life. It means focusing on the positives in any situation rather than the negatives. It means thinking well of yourself rather than constantly putting yourself down. It means thinking well of others, dealing with them in a positive way. It means expecting the best from the world, trusting it will provide.

◀ **Living with positivity**
Positive thinkers look back on the past with satisfaction rather than regret, and into the future with optimism and hope.

CREATING A POSITIVE WORLD

To start thinking positively, it is important to realize that the way you experience something is determined by what you think about it. It may appear that events are intrinsically happy or sad, but in fact it is your responses that make them feel good or bad, pleasurable or painful. If you face the world with pessimism, cynicism, and self-criticism, you will experience life as negative; if you respond with optimism, excitement, and confidence, you will create a cycle of positivity that builds your energy and inspires others.

Amy reacts calmly, so Tim apologizes, and the relationship is strengthened

Amy thinks positively and reminds herself that it was an accident

Tim reacts defensively, and the friendship is damaged

▲ **Responding to events**
Tim has broken Amy's vase. By reacting in a positive way, Amy can prevent an argument and preserve the friendship.

Amy responds angrily and accuses Tim of being clumsy

Fact File

Studies made in 1953, 1984, 1990, 1993, and 2002 suggest that positive thinkers are more likely than negative people to stay healthy into middle age and to have successful careers. They are half as likely to quit their jobs, 30 times more likely to be happy – and on average add 7.5 years to their life span.

APPRECIATING POSITIVITY

Positive thinking means keeping sufficiently balanced in your awareness of problems to stay motivated, able to take action, and feel good about what you are doing. This does not mean you should ignore difficulties or be relentlessly optimistic. Ideally you should register problems – perhaps a bad day at work or an upset with your partner – and then, instead of getting locked in paralyzing loops of bad feeling, move quickly to take action to solve those difficulties.

Recognizing the Signs

Your mental approach to life is a combination of your feelings, thoughts, and beliefs. Identifying and distinguishing these three elements is the first crucial step that you must take if you are to shift your outlook from negative to positive.

BECOMING AWARE OF YOUR FEELINGS

The most basic indicators of your positivity or negativity are your emotions. The more aware you are of emotional signals, the more you will be able to move your feelings from negative to positive. Learn to recognize the physical sensations that accompany your emotions. For example, you may be aware of anxious butterflies in your stomach or excited tingles down your spine. Register the different responses that you have to your emotions, perhaps losing your temper when you feel irritated or being more generous than usual when contented.

Believing in yourself ▶

The positive belief, "I can be good at sport" prompts the thought, "I can win", and this motivates and energizes you into effective action. Your success generates positive expectations, reinforcing your self-belief and boosting your abilities.

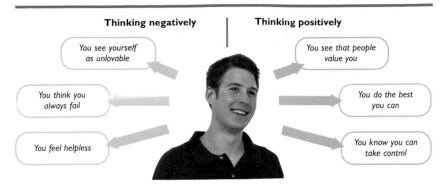

Thinking negatively

You see yourself as unlovable

You think you always fail

You feel helpless

Thinking positively

You see that people value you

You do the best you can

You know you can take control

▲ **Choosing positivity**
There are always two ways of thinking about anything in life – negatively or positively. The choice is yours.

66 What lies behind us and what lies before us are tiny matters compared to what lies within us. 99

Ralph Waldo Emerson

UNDERSTANDING BELIEFS

At the bedrock of your thinking are beliefs, deep-rooted ideas that are the result of your experiences. These are not necessarily religious beliefs, but life attitudes – convictions that colour your world view. Whereas thoughts are relative, beliefs tend to feel completely true, undeniable, and absolute. A negative belief can undermine your joy in life, but – because beliefs are fundamental to your thinking – if you analyze a negative belief and turn it into a positive belief, your whole approach to life becomes confident.

IDENTIFYING YOUR THOUGHTS

When events trigger your emotions, there is always an accompanying thought. You may experience this as an inner image, a sound, or a "self-talk" phrase, such as, "I am scared about this interview"…, "He is angry with me"…, "I bet the train is cancelled again". A thought may be about what happens in the present, a memory of the past, or a prediction of the future. The core strategy of positive thinking is to adapt these thoughts, emphasizing the positive and defusing the negative. Alter your thoughts and you automatically alter your emotions and redirect your actions.

At a Glance

● You need to distinguish your feelings, thoughts, and beliefs.

● A positive thought creates a positive feeling, and motivates positive action.

● Your feelings, thoughts, and beliefs can be shifted from negative to positive.

● A positive belief influences your whole approach to life.

Analyzing Your Approach

Tracking your thoughts, feelings, and beliefs helps you feel in control. It lets you understand why you are having negative thoughts. If you keep a record of your emotions, you can use it to gauge how successfully you are changing your attitude.

FOCUS POINT

● Monitor your progress in a daily diary – this will make you think and act more positively.

CATCHING THE THOUGHT

The most fundamental elements to track are your thoughts. If you find yourself feeling negative, take a few moments to relax, then register what comes into your head, and gather information about the way your mind is working. Take a mental snapshot of your thoughts. What pictures are you visualizing? What sounds are you hearing? What words are you saying to yourself? What memories of the past or fantasies of the future come to mind? Express your thought in one short sentence, such as "I will never get this right" or "I am really annoyed with him".

Keeps eyes closed to help concentration

▲ **Pinpointing your thoughts**
Capturing a negative thought is the first step in changing it. Concentrate exclusively on what is going on in your mind.

Useful Exercises

▶ Find early photographs to help you remember your childhood and recall the beliefs that you gained then.

▶ List three important people in your life. Ask what beliefs, negative and positive, they have passed on to you.

▶ To focus your mind on an angry or anxious thought, ask yourself "What is it that I am angry…worried about?"

AUDITING YOUR BELIEFS

To identify the beliefs that underlie your thoughts, learn to notice which negative thoughts crop up again and again. When you have a clear sense of that pattern, ask yourself, "What does this thought mean about me?" Answer with the words, "It means…". Then keep asking what your answer means about you until you reach an absolute statement, such as, "I am weak", "People are untrustworthy", or, "The world is a nasty place". Such definitive statements are your core beliefs about yourself and the world; identifying them enables you to challenge them.

KEEPING A DAILY THOUGHT DIARY

To understand how your thoughts affect your moods, create a "thought diary" in which you make a written account of your approach to life. In a notebook, write down each thought, with the circumstances that gave rise to it. Next, think about the effect that the thought had on you and write this down too. Look back over this diary at the end of each day, to analyze whether your thoughts and feelings triggered helpful or unhelpful actions. If you reread the diary once a week, you can use the entries to trace your thought patterns, gauge how successfully you are making improvements, and spot where you need to make extra effort.

▼ **Quantifying your moods**
A daily diary allows you to take an in-depth look at your moods. Record each situation as it occurs, and your response to it – with a score to indicate how strong the emotion was – and note what the effects were.

Self-Talk

As you begin to trace negative thought patterns, try using sentences like these to analyze what lies behind them and how you might use them positively.

❝ *I know what triggered this thought and I can find a positive alternative.* ❞

❝ *This negative thought is an opportunity to work out what is important to me.* ❞

❝ *This thought will help me to analyze my perceptions of other people and decide whether they are valid.* ❞

❝ *Just because I sometimes have negative thoughts, it does not mean that I am a negative person.* ❞

Diary entry begins with what happened to trigger a mood

Emotion aroused is identified

Positive or negative reaction is recorded

Situation	Thought	Emotion	Emotion Score	Reaction	Result
11:15 a.m. boss criticized report	I will never satisfy him	anger, hopelessness	6	snapped at colleague	had bad day
18:30 p.m. met Sam	I have some great friends	happiness	9	relaxed and enjoyed myself	slept well

Positive or negative thought is noted down

Strength of emotion is scored out of 10

Overall result completes entry

How Positive Are You?

Just how positive are you in your life? Respond to the following statements by marking the answers that are closest to your experience. Be as honest as you can: if your answer is "Never", mark Option 1; if it is "Always", mark Option 4; and so on. Add your scores together, and refer to the analysis to estimate your current positivity.

Options	
1	Never
2	Occasionally
3	Frequently
4	Always

How Do You Respond?

	1	2	3	4
1 I find it hard to be positive.	☐	☐	☐	☐
2 I feel life is out to get me.	☐	☐	☐	☐
3 When bad things happen, I go under.	☐	☐	☐	☐
4 I can think myself into feeling bad.	☐	☐	☐	☐
5 I always imagine the worst.	☐	☐	☐	☐
6 I find myself talking negatively.	☐	☐	☐	☐
7 I feel I am not worth it.	☐	☐	☐	☐
8 Other people fail my expectations.	☐	☐	☐	☐
9 I think the world is a dangerous place.	☐	☐	☐	☐

	1	2	3	4
10 I suffer from painful memories.	☐	☐	☐	☐
11 I find it difficult to accept compliments.	☐	☐	☐	☐
12 I believe I am not much good.	☐	☐	☐	☐
13 I get overwhelmed by bad feeling.	☐	☐	☐	☐
14 I often feel very angry.	☐	☐	☐	☐
15 I cannot get what I want in life.	☐	☐	☐	☐
16 I get anxious about things.	☐	☐	☐	☐
17 People say I am pessimistic.	☐	☐	☐	☐
18 It is difficult to enjoy myself.	☐	☐	☐	☐

	1	2	3	4		1	2	3	4
19 I am lacking in confidence.	☐	☐	☐	☐	**26** I feel I am not in control of my life.	☐	☐	☐	☐
20 I have no motivation to do things.	☐	☐	☐	☐	**27** My love life is unsatisfactory.	☐	☐	☐	☐
21 My life lacks purpose and meaning.	☐	☐	☐	☐	**28** I do not find my job fulfilling.	☐	☐	☐	☐
22 My surroundings feel uncomfortable.	☐	☐	☐	☐	**29** I do not think I achieve much.	☐	☐	☐	☐
23 I frequently feel unwell.	☐	☐	☐	☐	**30** A bad day can really throw me.	☐	☐	☐	☐
24 I am unsupported by others.	☐	☐	☐	☐	**31** I lurch from crisis to crisis.	☐	☐	☐	☐
25 My lifestyle is constantly stressful.	☐	☐	☐	☐	**32** I am not happy being the age I am.	☐	☐	☐	☐

Analysis

When you have added up your scores, look at the analysis below to establish how positive you are at present. Then make a note of the areas where you are most and least positive. As you read through the book, work particularly on your weak areas.

32–64 You have an extremely positive attitude. Build on that and your life will be even happier and more effective.

65–95 You are generally positive about life. But you could do even better if, with this book, you improved your approach.

96–128 Your positivity levels are worryingly low. Use this book to develop useful mental strategies and find support to become more positive.

My weakest areas are:

_____
_____
_____
_____

My strongest areas are:

_____
_____
_____
_____

Learning to Be Positive

To improve your approach to life, you must ensure every aspect of your behaviour is positive. Examine and, if necessary, change your thoughts, your beliefs, and your view of yourself.

Challenging Your Thoughts

The key to real success in positive thinking is to find as many ways as possible in which to challenge the validity of your negative thoughts, and then to replace those thoughts with others that are more positive and more realistic.

RETHINKING YOUR THOUGHTS

To turn negative thoughts into positive ones, you have to realize that they are distortions of reality. Nothing is ever all bad; it is only your defensive thinking that makes it seem so. So get into the habit of analyzing your thoughts to see where you have misinterpreted things and therefore where your negativities are misplaced. Rebalancing thoughts like this creates a shift of emotion and starts you thinking differently long-term – and so has a deep-rooted effect on your approach to life.

▲ **Acknowledging negativity**
Look at your thought diary, and you may see that in the past you have distorted a thought negatively. Learn to look for a more balanced response.

CHECKING THE FACTS

As soon as you become aware of a negative thought, challenge its validity. It may be that your observations were wrong, or you misunderstood what really happened. So, question events. Check information with an objective source. For example, was your colleague correct to predict redundancies, or was she dramatizing? A problem you thought you saw may well turn out to be non-existent.

▼ **Confirming your judgement**
This man has heard a disturbing rumour about his son's behaviour. Realizing that his negative thoughts may be unfounded, he checks out the facts with his son.

Father asks son about a rumour he has heard

Son has evidence that proves the rumour is false

▼ **Shifting misplaced negativity**
Look at your thought diary and rethink one of your negative thoughts positively. Note the new, positive emotion, score its strength, and compare this score with that of the old, negative emotion.

REVIEWING YOUR TRACK RECORD

You can probably remember a time when you expected the worst, only to find things turned out for the best. Being aware of this will help you challenge any negative thoughts you are having now and will remind you of a tendency to think negatively. Acknowledge that your judgement has been wrong before, and you will more easily accept that you might be wrong this time as well.

Diary entry is chosen for the rethinking exercise

Score given to strength of original emotion is noted

Situation	Thought	Emotion	Score	Rethink	New Emotion	Score
11:15 a.m. boss criticized report	I'll never satisfy him	anger, hopelessness	6	he's usually pleased with my work	more hopeful	8

Original pessimistic response is registered

New, positive reaction is written into diary

New, positive emotion is identified

Strength of new emotion scores higher than old emotion

BEING REALISTIC

It is natural to want to be perfect, but aiming for perfection inevitably leads to negative feelings simply because – in work, play, friendship, or love – perfection just is not possible most of the time. So challenge your perfectionist thoughts. Be realistic in what you expect of yourself, of other people, of the world. Do not stop aiming high, achieving well, or expecting the best of others, but stop feeling bad when things do fall short of perfection in some way.

Doing the best you can ▶

It is important not to feel you have failed if, for example, you do not get that hole in one. Be content with setting yourself a target you can achieve – and enjoy the game.

FOCUS POINTS

● Avoid projecting your problems into the future: in the end all things pass.

● Recognize when you are distorting thoughts. Step back and think of a more balanced response instead.

KEEPING THINGS IN PERSPECTIVE

Even when a situation is truly bad, you can avoid becoming overwhelmed by negativity. To do this, you need to stop focusing on problem areas and concentrate on the good ones. So, bring to the front of your mind elements that turned out well. Focus on the positives rather than generalizing the negatives. Check for signs that you are exaggerating the difficulties, and remember that just because one element of your life goes wrong, it does not mean it all will.

Things to Do	Things to Avoid
✔ Do be your own advocate; spring to the defence when you start to criticize yourself.	✗ Avoid black-and-white thinking; if something is bad, do not think everything is bad, all the time, for ever.
✔ Do make allowances for error; it is fine to be tired, inattentive, or off-form occasionally.	✗ Avoid discounting the positive; if you do something good, register it and do not push it aside.
✔ Do be sure to look at the big picture, rather than focusing on one tiny detail that may be negative.	✗ Avoid instant judgements; take time to think things through before you decide that they are negative.

Finding a Balanced Response

Thought Distortion	Sample Trigger	Negative Thought	More Balanced Thought
Interpreting things as bad	Your boss is not interested in you.	"She is not pleased with me."	"She is under a lot of pressure."
Imagining problems	Your partner frowns.	"What have I done wrong?"	"I wonder why he is frowning."
Making generalizations	A friend forgets your birthday.	"No one likes me."	"I got lots of other cards."
Imagining the worst will happen	The sales figures are down.	"We are going to go bust!"	"How can we get more sales?"
Exaggerating negatives	You scrape the car on the gatepost.	"The whole world is against me!"	"Oops, scraped the car!"

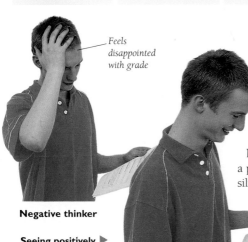

Feels disappointed with grade

Negative thinker

Seeing positively ▶
When you are given feedback, or exam results, for example, focus on the successful element rather than the negative aspect.

Knows he did his best – whatever his grade

Positive thinker

LOOKING ON THE BRIGHT SIDE

The Chinese word for problem also means opportunity. The lesson here is to challenge negative thoughts by looking for the opportunity that lies within a problem. Maybe you learned a lesson, gained motivation, avoided a problem? Train yourself to look for a silver lining, even in small difficulties.

Altering Your Mental Images

Thoughts can be experienced as mental representations: internal pictures, sounds, and words. By exploring, shifting, and developing these, you can affect the way you think and feel about both yourself and your life.

MAKING POSITIVE PICTURES

To feel more positive in the short term, try changing the content of your mental images. Change by adding: see your scary boss with spotty underpants over his trousers. Take away: in a stressful and hectic office, picture your desk on a sunny, deserted beach. See behind a façade: hear your worst enemy confessing how insecure he or she is. Put up a barrier: think of yourself surrounded by a bubble that protects you from problems. The things you envisage in your mind's eye will not automatically happen, but changing your inner view of reality will make you feel better and more able to achieve a good outcome.

FOCUS POINT

● Understand that you cannot change reality, but you can change your preception of it – and so achieve positive results.

● Remember that when using visualization you can control what you see.

▲ **Changing the scene**
When you are feeling rushed in a busy supermarket, imagine it empty of people and trollies – you will feel calmer.

Useful Exercises

▶ To improve your mood, try altering the style in which you experience internal images.

▶ If someone is angry, envisage their face soft-focused. It may make you feel less threatened.

▶ If you find your inner voice is slow and lethargic talk to yourself quickly, to raise your energy.

▶ Practise using visualization to allow previously unrecognized thoughts to emerge.

TAPPING YOUR UNCONSCIOUS

Visualization involves allowing your mental images to extend into a kind of internal video. This technique is useful if you want to make a decision, envisage a goal, or take the first step towards achieving an aim. Playing out a situation in your mind can raise your creativity, change your emotional state, help you focus, or reduce tension. Create a clear image of what you want to explore, then run the video, noticing what happens and how you feel. If what you are seeing starts to feel negative, let the images go and slowly return to the present: speed your breathing up, stretch, and open your eyes.

Sara imagines herself revising regularly and effectively

Stays in control of images

Using visualization ▶
With exams looming, Sara wants to feel calm and in control. She plays out positive scenes, and by the end she is feeling relaxed and energized.

Sits comfortably and relaxes

Making Internal Images Positive

Style	Questions to Ask	Positivity Technique
Size	How big are the images you see?	Enlarge positive images, diminish negative images.
Distance	How far away is the image?	Move positives closer, move negatives further away.
Focus	Is the image sharp or soft?	Soften the focus to relax yourself, sharpen the focus to motivate.
Colour	Are you seeing in colour or black-and-white?	Try adding, softening, and brightening colour to increase energy and enthusiasm.
Viewpoint	Are you in the scene or an observer?	Imagine yourself inside positive scenes, but standing outside negative ones.
Movement	Are objects moving or still?	Speed up images to energize, slow them down to calm yourself.

Using Constructive Language

Your language not only reflects your behaviour, but also influences it. Therefore, to succeed in living a positive life, you must choose and use positive words and phrases. So, examine and, if necessary, change the words you use.

CHOOSING THE RIGHT WORDS

Be aware of the words and phrases you naturally use. If necessary, ask others to tell you what expressions you use. Then identify those that you use when you are being self-critical, pessimistic, or problem-focused. For each, generate a positive alternative. Then, when you hear yourself using a pessimistic phrase, stop in mid-sentence and switch to the more optimistic one. In time you will spot when you are talking negatively, and automatically correct what you are saying.

Self-Talk

If you have a work problem, such as a promotion you feel nervous about, try wording statements on the following lines and repeating them to yourself regularly.

❝I will take this as a reflection of how people value me.❞

❝I can master the new skills and responsibilities involved.❞

❝I can enlist the help of my team, and at the same time look after my own needs.❞

▼ **Rephrasing your language**
Learn to recognize when you are using negative, powerless words or phrases, and get into the habit of replacing them with more positive, powerful ones.

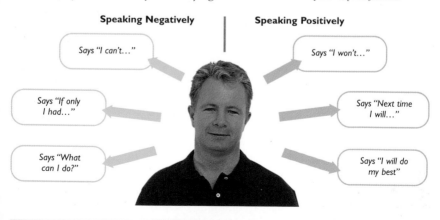

Speaking Negatively

Says "I can't..."

Says "If only I had..."

Says "What can I do?"

Speaking Positively

Says "I won't..."

Says "Next time I will..."

Says "I will do my best"

AVOIDING "SHOULD"

You probably use phrases such as, "I should…", "I should not…", "I must…", "I ought not to" when you want to do something different from what you are doing. But by using these words you imply that your current course of action is mistaken or quite simply bad – and that is likely to make you feel demotivated, anxious, resentful. Analyze why you find it hard to change. You may find good reasons for your current behaviour and decide to carry on as before. But if you want to change, try using phrases such as, "I would get further if I…", "I intend to…", I want to…".

FOCUS POINTS

● To help you maintain your positive language, ask friends to challenge you whenever you start talking negatively.

● Make a list of positive words and use them, one per day, until they are part of your normal vocabulary.

Grandfather's affirmation about spending time with family becomes self-fulfilling

66 Kindness in words creates confidence. Kindness in thinking creates profoundness. 99

Lao Tzu

USING AFFIRMATIONS

Affirmations are phrases that encapsulate the good side of life: "I am happy" or "People love me". Affirmations imprint positive beliefs on your subconscious, and by doing so can help you achieve a goal. To create an affirmation, first decide what your aim is. Express that briefly, so that you remember it easily. Word it in the present tense, so that your unconscious realizes that you want action now. Then repeat your affirmation, with energy, at regular intervals, until it takes effect.

◀ **Aiming for the best in life**
Identify your aim, such as spending more time with your family. Express this affirmation in a few words, repeat it, keep it in the front of your mind, and you are likely to make it come into effect.

21

Rethinking Your Beliefs

B*eliefs are firm convictions resulting from your experiences in life. The best leave you feeling positive about yourself, other people, and the world; the worst leave you feeling powerless. Identify helpful beliefs, and learn to change those that are not.*

66 Nothing is a waste of time if you use the experience wisely. **99**

Rodin

BUILDING POSITIVE BELIEFS

Strengthen your useful and supportive beliefs by noticing whatever confirms them. For example, your belief is, "People really value me": over the next week or so note down every time someone does or says something to support this. Notice when people ask for your opinion. Accept when people compliment you. Remember times when someone tells you are important. Ignore any feelings about being unvalued – these are no just feelings. Look at the actual evidence.

FOCUS POINTS

● Ask yourself what you are afraid of, then check if your fear is really founded.

● Opt for experiences that challenge your fears. Do a course and master something that scares you.

▲ **Accepting positive feedback**
When you talk to your friends, notice how they enjoy your company and value your opinions. Registering others' positivity about you will raise your self-belief.

COLLECTING THE PROOF

If you struggle to convince yourself about a belief such as, "People value me", get a friend or partner to tell you the ways in which they admire you. Or in a work appraisal, ask your manager to list the ways you are valued. Talk to others about whether they feel valued. It is likely you will find they feel as insecure as you do, however confident they seem, and you will realize you are not alone.

SETTING UP EXPERIMENTS

Test your core beliefs. For example, to prove, "People value me", you might ask ten friends to do you a favour. Your fear may be that they will all turn you down, but most likely the news will be better than you expect. If six friends respond well, you will have proved that a majority of people do value you, and you can take on that positive belief. (If all ten do say no, consider making changes with the help of a counsellor.)

At a Glance

- Noticing when people show respect for your opinion will boost your self-belief.

- Asking other people's opinions helps you consolidate positive beliefs about yourself.

- Rethinking core beliefs has a positive effect on behaviour.

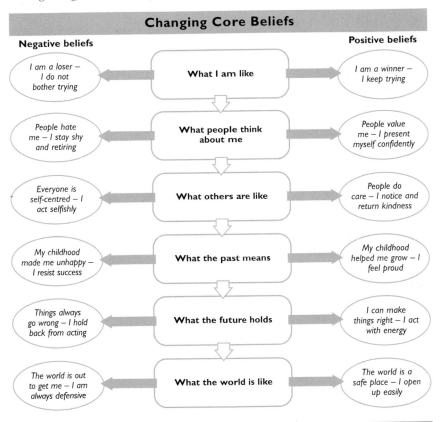

Changing Core Beliefs

Negative beliefs | Positive beliefs

Negative beliefs		Positive beliefs
I am a loser – I do not bother trying	**What I am like**	I am a winner – I keep trying
People hate me – I stay shy and retiring	**What people think about me**	People value me – I present myself confidently
Everyone is self-centred – I act selfishly	**What others are like**	People do care – I notice and return kindness
My childhood made me unhappy – I resist success	**What the past means**	My childhood helped me grow – I feel proud
Things always go wrong – I hold back from acting	**What the future holds**	I can make things right – I act with energy
The world is out to get me – I am always defensive	**What the world is like**	The world is a safe place – I open up easily

Establishing Self-Esteem

People who have high self-esteem are natural positive thinkers. And having a positive outlook means having high self-esteem. It follows that if you use positive thinking techniques to enhance your core beliefs, your self-esteem will soar.

Assessing Your Self-Esteem Level

How high is your self-esteem? Tick any of the following statements that you think describe you correctly.

● I am not truly happy with who I am. ☐

● I find it difficult to accept being told I have done well. ☐

● If something goes wrong, I tend to think I am to blame. ☐

● I find it difficult to ask for what I want in life. ☐

Analysis The more ticks there are, the lower your self-esteem. It is easier to adopt positive thinking strategies if you feel good about yourself.

Turning your back on criticism ▶
Disassociate yourself from criticism and accept the appreciation of others without embarassment or excuses.

RETHINKING THE MESSAGES

The more positive the judgements others make about you, the better you feel about yourself; the more negative their judgements, the worse you feel. The most crucial step in feeling good about yourself is realizing that no one can make you feel bad unless you let them. So, distance yourself from those who criticize you. Instead, take on board other people's gratitude and praise.

Turns to friends who give praise, ignoring those who criticize

Compliments friend and is appreciated

Acknowledge when
things go wrong

⇩

Consider how to tackle
the problem

⇩

Take action to
solve the problem

⇩

Begin to create
an improvement

⇩

Confirm own ability
to sort out problems

⇩

Feel good about
yourself

⇩

Take
further action

⇩

Create further
improvements

▲ **Riding high on self-esteem**
Self-esteem can trigger a spiral of good or bad feeling, according to how high or low it is. If it is low, the slightest problem will trigger negativity. With high self-esteem, you can cope with any difficulties that arise: acknowledge the problem, and your confidence will set you on the right path.

SETTING YOUR OWN TARGETS

If you largely succeed in what you expect of yourself, your self-esteem will be solid. So, aim only as high as you can realistically reach, rather than thinking you ought to be perfect. In the same way, do not aim so low that you under-achieve. When you do succeed, congratulate yourself. Avoid comparing yourself against others; everyone has their own strengths and weaknesses. Set your own expectations and judge your achievement by your improvement.

▲ **Being your own best friend**
Treat yourself as you would treat a good friend. So congratulate yourself on any successes – however small they may be – and invite friends or colleagues to share your celebrations.

BEING KIND TO YOURSELF

If you were supporting someone who had low self-esteem, you would not criticize them and put them down. Yet you may give yourself a hard time in just that way. Be fair to yourself, and offer yourself the same kindness as you would instinctively offer a friend. Moment to moment, during the day, point out what you are doing right. Yes, be realistic about your limitations, but forgive yourself for any failures. Encourage yourself to learn lessons from your own mistakes.

Maintaining Positive Behaviour

To integrate positive-thinking strategies fully into your life, you must learn to apply them in all circumstances, at all times. Only when they are second nature will you really reap the benefits.

Starts the day by mentally listing the things that are going well at work

STAYING ON TRACK

Under stress you may find your positivity starts to slip. If this happens, distract yourself by concentrating on what is happening around you. Repeat an affirmation, smile to create a feelgood physiology, or give yourself a break by being determinedly negative for a whole ten minutes. And, if you find yourself being gloomy in order to get sympathy, find other, more cheerful ways of getting attention.

▲ **Focusing on the positive**
Pick a time of day – perhaps first thing in the morning or after work – where for just a few minutes you sit quietly and focus on the good things in your life. Make a habit of doing this daily to maintain a positive attitude.

FOCUS POINT

● Aim to increase the high spots of your life and decrease the low. This will help you to focus on the positivity in what you do.

● Practise the positive-thinking strategies until you are using them easily and without effort.

KEEPING UP THE PRACTICE

The more positive you are, the more positive you learn to be. Expand the positive-thinking opportunities in your life. During the day pick a task, an interaction, or a journey where you focus on thinking and being positive. Catch yourself every time you slip into negativity and consciously replace that with a positive thought. Once you start to succeed, designate areas of your life as negative-free zones, where you only feel, think, and act positively. Start with the most stress-free areas of your life and gradually expand your positivity throughout all areas of your life.

USING "AS IF" APPROACHES

If you meet a major challenge to your positivity, try acting "as if" everything is fine. Act as if you like yourself, or as if you accept others; act as if your future is bright, or as if your past is resolved. Picture yourself as successful, beautiful, effective, loving – and whatever you say or do, make it the words or action of the person you want to be. This approach may feel false at first, but you will learn valuable lessons about what it means to be positive, and with practice will grow into the role.

Useful Exercises

▶ Each day, note something you have done, rate it one to 10 according to how you enjoyed it, and give reasons.

▶ Each week choose at least three positive things to do for yourself.

▶ Each month, allow yourself one day of total indulgence, doing only things you enjoy.

Self-Talk

If you find yourself becoming negative and feel frustrated with harmful thinking patterns, use these instant self-talk boosters to raise your mood and keep yourself on track.

❝I am improving day-to-day, even if I still have negative thoughts sometimes.❞

❝I am making a conscious effort to do more of what I enjoy and less of what I do not enjoy.❞

❝My negative thought is a reminder that I need to be kinder to myself.❞

PLANNING A POSITIVE DAY

A good way to get into the habit of thinking positively all day and every day is to make a day plan. Write down at least ten possibilities for specific times of day, from waking in the morning to falling asleep at night. They might be: 7 a.m. – shower, repeat positive affirmations; 7.45 a.m. – really enjoy breakfast; 9 a.m. – write positive affirmation and place on desk; 11 a.m. – take relaxing break or go for quiet walk; 12.30 p.m. – read something enjoyable over lunch; 6 p.m. – spend evening with positive people; 7.30 p.m. – enjoy good meal; 11.45 p.m. – repeat a final affirmation before falling asleep.

▼ **Indulging yourself**
Your day plan should include entries for the evening – perhaps taking a long, indulgent bath listening to relaxing music.

Relaxes with fragrant bath oil

Fulfilling Your Potential

To be truly effective in life, apply positive-thinking strategies not only to day-to-day thoughts, actions, and emotions, but also at a deeper level, to firmly ingrained character traits.

Working with Emotions

E motions are the first signals generated by your body and mind when there is something in your life to which you need to pay attention. Catch negative emotions quickly, at source, and use the energy they generate to motivate you to action.

FOCUS POINT

● Take control of your emotions – you will then be able to look at a problem rationally.

▲ **Turning emotions around**
You can learn to channel the emotional energy expended in anger, for example, into love – and so build a stronger relationship.

ACKNOWLEDGING EMOTIONS

You might think the best way to be positive is to ignore painful emotions. But this is not so. Your emotions make their presence felt for a reason. They are indicative of an increase in your body's energy levels, triggered to deal with a threat – your partner's anger, your sense of failure, your boss's disapproval. Unless you acknowledge them, your emotions will intensify to the point where you are forced to pay attention. When you feel a negative emotion, stop and register it momentarily, then explore why you are feeling it. Appreciate that it is giving you energy to cope.

Things to Do	Things to Avoid
✓ Do distract your attention from "inside" emotions to the world "outside" by focusing on things around you.	✗ Avoid bottling up negative emotions. If you feel furious, go and play a ball-game to let your anger out.
✓ Do work off emotionally induced adrenalin by taking physical exercise.	✗ Avoid thinking you are not permitted to feel down occasionally.
✓ Do talk through your feelings with someone who is able to listen carefully.	✗ Avoid wallowing in an emotion. Instead, take action to solve the problem.

CALMING YOURSELF

Once you have acknowledged your emotions, use calming techniques to lift yourself into a state where you can start to think clearly. First calm yourself physically by sitting comfortably, closing your eyes, and taking three deep, slow breaths from your stomach. Then calm yourself mentally, by concentrating, for example, on saying the words of your favourite song or counting back from 100. Once you are calm, you will find it easier to focus your mind and so be better able to cope with whatever problem you have.

Takes mind off problem and thinks calm thoughts

Finds a quiet place to sit comfortably

◄ **Taking control**
A 20-minute break from an emotional situation allows your physiology to return to normal.

At a Glance

• Negative emotions must be explored, not ignored.

• The energy you put into an emotion can be diverted into coping with the cause of it.

• Calming yourself allows you to focus your mind on dealing with your problem.

• You can take control of your emotions, rather than letting them control you.

RELEASING PAIN

When a painful emotion is strong or lingering, defuse it by actively experiencing it. Mentally describe your feelings to yourself. Or find a quiet place, then actively shout or cry. Go further: deliberately exaggerate the feeling, and be as negative as you can for a while. As you start to feel better, note how long you have been expressing your emotion, then – strange as this advice may seem – carry on expressing it for at least as long again. Learn that emotions do fade once you really express them, and that you, rather than the emotions, are in control.

Managing Your Feelings

Some emotions are more challenging than others, and can deeply affect your self-esteem and your relationships. Develop ways to manage them actively day-to-day, and do not hold back from getting expert help if they begin to overwhelm you.

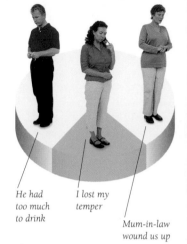

He had too much to drink

I lost my temper

Mum-in-law wound us up

▲ Defusing guilt
You may feel last night's argument was all down to you. But a cold, hard look may show that responsibility is more evenly divided and that you need not take all the blame.

PUTTING GUILT IN PERSPECTIVE

Guilt is criticism directed inwards because you feel you have acted wrongly. It can be useful. If you feel guilt before taking one particular decision or action, stop and rethink; if you feel guilt after the event, consider making amends. But if you feel guilty about everything, or cannot let go of self-blame about the past, there is something very wrong. So, try imagining the guilt-inducing event as if it had happened to someone else; with this more objective perspective, consider to what extent you were responsible and whether you really need to feel guilty.

Useful Exercises

▶ To help anger die away, breathe slowly and deeply.

▶ If you are angry with someone, use imagination to see them as a fictional character, whose actions do not hurt you.

▶ As part of mastering the art of assertiveness, practise summarizing a point you would like to make in no more than five words.

HANDLING ANGER

Anger is criticism turned outwards because you feel others have acted wrongly. If someone actively threatens you, anger is useful because it prepares you for self-defence. But if you are angry only because someone does not meet your expectations, then it just makes you and other people unhappy. Instead, adapt your expectations to be more realistic. Understand why the other person cannot meet your standards. Ask them to change what they are doing. Try walking away, returning when you are calmer. If none of these ideas work, just let your anger go, and move on.

UNDERSTANDING ASSERTIVENESS

When you are in conflict with someone, you need something from them, or they are denying your rights, it may seem as if the only way out of the situation is to back down or to fight for your rights. But there is a third way. An assertive approach means being adult about your needs and your wants, neither giving up nor being oppressive. It means knowing you have the right to ask for what you need and to be heard. It also suggests ways of achieving that. Assertiveness is not a one-way ticket. You need to be prepared to listen to the other person, recognize their point of view, and negotiate a win–win solution.

At a Glance

● Seeing who else is involved will help you let go of guilt.

● You may be able to dissipate anger just by taking a break.

● Assertiveness means valuing others' needs, as well as yours.

● An assertive statement is succinct and avoids blame.

Keeps eye contact, and is respectful but direct

Demands and attacks

Avoids eye contact, and hesitates

Aggressive

Passive

Assertive

▲ Looking assertive

Make sure that your body language reflects your assertive – rather than aggressive or passively guilty – approach.

FOCUS POINT

● If you have made a mistake, acknowledge your error, and apologize to the person you have offended.

ACTING ASSERTIVELY

Think through what you need to say, then make a simple, short statement of what happened, your feelings, and your preferred solution: "When you took credit for my idea, I felt belittled and angry. I would like you to tell the boss it was me who did the work." Choose a quiet time and place to raise the issue. Neither attack nor apologize. If the other person argues or gets upset, repeat your statement calmly. This will make it easier for them to take it on board and start negotiating a solution.

COPING WITH ANXIETY

Anxiety alerts you to a difficulty that you think you need to solve. Some worry is natural in everyone's life, so do not expect to be entirely free of tension all the time. However, particularly when you are under stress, you may find your anxiety level never drops. To avoid this, learn to make a clear distinction between what you can solve and what you cannot solve, what is your responsibility and what is not. Learn that there are some things that simply are not your problem. But when something is your problem you must take action immediately to shift the downward spiral of anxiety to the positive.

Relieving Anxiety

Recognize feeling of anxiety

⬇

Tell yourself to relax

⬇

Breathe slowly and deeply

⬇

Relax your whole body

⬇

Feel calmer

⬇

Become more rational

⬇

Feel even calmer

⬇

Begin to feel in control

Does not allow suspicion to undermine self-worth

Is careful to express loving feelings

▲ **Building up security**

If you have suspicions about your partner, recognize the feeling, but do not allow anxiety to preoccupy you. Express loving, positive feelings, and have faith in yourself and your relationship.

AVOIDING JEALOUSY

A feeling of jealousy may alert you to a genuine threat to your relationship. But such feelings can get out of control, so you feel jealous without reason. If you find yourself inappropriately suspicious, the answer is not to keep a closer watch on your partner; it is to build your self-belief. That way, you believe that you are worth your partner's love, and start to feel secure. And, if the worst does happen, and your relationship fails, your self-belief will allow you to recover and move on.

LIVING THROUGH YOUR GRIEF

All loss – for example, bereavement, relationship break-up, or redundancy – creates in your mind and body a natural but painful mourning process. So get practical support, particularly when shock first sets in. After that, express your emotions, even unhappy ones; you will recover more quickly if you allow yourself to feel the grief. As time passes, be sure to find someone to whom you can talk about your feelings. In the longer term, honour the memory of what you have lost – a relative, a friend, or even a job you have enjoyed, laying to rest the bad times and remembering the good.

▼ **Talking through your loss**
Share your loss and allow yourself to grieve, rather than carrying on regardless. Only when you have come through the cycle of grieving can you begin to feel positive again.

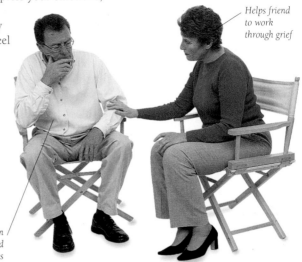

Helps friend to work through grief

Talks to a person who has experienced a similar loss

The Six-Stage Cycle of Grieving

Stage	Reactions	What Will Help
Shock	Shakiness, loss of control.	Practical support.
Denial	Cutting off from emotions.	Time and patience.
Grief	Sadness, tears.	Ability to cry.
Anger	Bitterness and self-blame.	Acceptance of anger as useful.
Depression	Hopelessness and helplessness.	Medication, counselling.
Resolution	Acceptance, moving on.	Support in re-engaging with life.

Creating Optimism

One of the fundamentals of positive thinking is its emphasis on being positive about the future. Take on this life approach fully and you are an optimist – someone who faces the future resourcefully, rather than feeling hopeless and helpless.

THINKING OPTIMISTICALLY

Optimists develop their life approach like this: they take credit for the good things that happen in their lives, but put the bad things down to circumstance, coincidence, or mistake. Hence they feel in charge and empowered. Pessimists take the blame for the bad but think the good is down to sheer chance, which leaves them feeling inadequate and powerless. To be an optimist, recognize the contribution you have made to a positive event, and congratulate yourself.

▲ **Staying on top**
Optimists feel in control of their lives and do not feel overwhelmed by the demands of others – even those put on a busy mother by her young family.

▲ **Making a start**
If you have a large task to undertake – decorating, for example – take it one step at a time. That way you feel in control.

TAKING ACTION

Optimists feel empowered even when faced with problem situations. The key to feeling optimistic about a problem is simply to take action. If you act, you will feel more hopeful because you are creating the chance that things will improve. So the minute you feel yourself beginning to slip into pessimism, do something – almost anything – to tackle whatever the problem is that is triggering your mood. Take one step and you will feel more hopeful. If that does not work, then be flexible: do something different. Your action does not need to solve things instantly. It just needs to remind you that you have taken charge and are on your way to making things better.

Assessing Your Optimism Level

How optimistic are you? Put a tick beside any of the following statements that you feel describe you accurately:

- I feel that things usually turn out for the best. ☐
- I always keep going in the face of obstacles. ☐
- When the going gets tough, I get going. ☐
- I do not give up hope. ☐
- I am the sort of person who manages to keep things in perspective. ☐
- I do not mind asking for help if I find a task difficult. ☐

The more boxes you have ticked, the more optimistic you are. Unticked boxes indicate a need to take action so you face the world more optimistically.

GATHERING RESOURCES

Optimism means feeling powerful, feeling you have the personal resources to achieve what you want to achieve. So in any problem situation, do an audit of what resources you have – your own talents and knowledge, sources of specialist expertise, friends, and family. Then identify what else you need in order to cope. Think of ways to fill those resource gaps – and set about doing so.

Identifies needs

Lists external resources

Brainstorms ways to solve problems

Notes personal skills

Seeks help where needed

▲ **Counting your assets**
Instead of feeling defeatist when confronted with a problem to be solved, optimists take charge, they work out where they need help, and then they go out and find it.

CONFRONTING PESSIMISM

If you tend to be pessimistic, remember that the outcome of any one issue usually falls midway between the most pessimistic and most optimistic predictions. So, when you have a problem, make a worst-case and a best-case prediction. When predicting the worst, you might ask, "How likely is it that this will happen?", "How can I reduce that likelihood?" When predicting the best, you may ask, "How likely is it that this will happen?" and "How can I maximize that likelihood?" Be realistic; what will probably happen is something between best and worst.

FOCUS POINTS

- Notice how optimists achieve more at work, are healthier, and suffer less depression than others.
- When predicting the outcome of a situation, ask how you can best achieve a good result, and what resources you need.

Developing the Feelgood Factor

To develop a really positive approach to life, do things that make you feel good. This not only makes you focus on living a contented life, it also builds your self-worth. Award yourself fun times, and give yourself the message that you deserve happiness.

LEARNING TO FEEL GOOD

Develop the habit of focusing minute-to-minute on something that you enjoy. Notice that particular sensation of physical relaxation that accompanies feelgood moments. Experience the pleasure in all five senses: what you see, hear, feel, taste, smell. Enhance your enjoyment by combining sensations, for example, playing uplifting music when reading a good book.

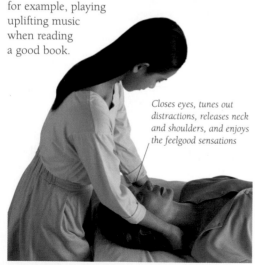

Closes eyes, tunes out distractions, releases neck and shoulders, and enjoys the feelgood sensations

Case Study

NAME: Tania
ISSUE: Lack of motivation
OBJECTIVE: To regain enthusiasm

Tania lives a busy life, with a full-time job as well as a lively five-year-old and a toddler to look after. She complains to her doctor of constant tiredness. He reassures her that she is perfectly healthy, but she still feels something is wrong. She cannot seem to summon the enthusiasm to do anything. Tania negotiates with her husband and her mother to look after the children one evening each week so she can attend a dance class. She also starts a programme of daily "treats" for herself – taking a stroll, writing an e-mail to her sister, watching a video. She begins by feeling a little guilty, but she perseveres. Within a month Tania is feeling more positive and energetic.

◀ **Enjoying the moment**
Treat yourself to a relaxing neck massage once in a while – and determine to indulge yourself more often.

▼ Having a laugh

Laughter is a good tonic: when you smile, your brainwave activity alters to parallel that of a happy person. So, even during a busy day, take the time to chat to a friend and share a joke.

Tells amusing story, and makes friend laugh

Relaxes as she laughs

GETTING LAUGHTER IN YOUR LIFE

Look for activities that produce the best physical experience of enjoyment: smiles and laughter. Smiling and laughing increases the body's positive endorphins and reduces stress hormones. Some believe it can heal, too. So smile at everyone you meet, tell jokes, read amusing books, tune in to comedy programmes, and mix with people who have a keen sense of humour.

INDULGING YOURSELF

Be energetic in seeking out good experiences. If the sun comes out, go for a walk; if that work project appeals, volunteer for it. Seize the day, indulge yourself. Realize that much of your time will be occupied with things you have not chosen or do not enjoy. By actively indulging yourself, you redress the balance towards enjoyment, daily life begins to seem more fun, and you feel positive in many different areas of your life.

▼ Adjusting the balance

Deliberately increase the amount of feelgood time in your life – particularly "me" time, where you can focus solely on yourself. Do an action-wheel to see how much of your 168 hours per week you allow for feelgood activities.

FOCUS POINTS

● Make time to play games and have fun. Buy your favourite childhood boardgame and play it with friends.

● Spend time with children when you can. They smile 400 times every day, as compared to a typical adult's 15 times.

Key: Hours per week

　Work and housework

　Commuting

　Sleeping and eating

　"Me" time

　Partner, friends, family

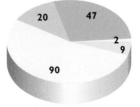

Low feelgood factor

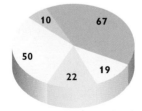

High feelgood factor

Building Confidence

*A*pply positive thinking to performance
and you gain confidence, whether
you are playing a sports match or facing
an interview. Positive thought patterns lie
at the heart of confidence; when you think
positively, you optimize your performance.

At a Glance

● Confident people remember
successes and forget failure.
Learn to put aside your
disappointments and focus
on your achievements.

● Before speaking publicly,
build confidence by rehearsing
until you can imagine yourself
performing successfully.

● Confident body language
will always give you an extra
physiological boost.

● To build long-term
confidence, balance your
learning experiences between
those where you are bound
to succeed and those where
you need to stretch yourself.

ERASING FAILURE

Confident people all share one simple mental
strategy. They concentrate on success but allow
memories of failure to fade. By all means note
where you went wrong, but do not dwell on your
mistakes, or become depressed by them. Simply
register them, and concentrate on what would
have been a better way to act. Then erase the
negative emotional charge by telling yourself that
failure is in the past and you are now a confident
person, who performs more effectively.

▼ **Congratulating yourself**
*After a performance such as giving a
presentation, congratulate yourself on
the areas where you did well.*

CONCENTRATING ON YOUR SUCCESS

After a big event such as a presentation or a
speech – or a practice session – go back and note
what you did correctly, and allow yourself to feel
good about that. Even if the best bits are only a
small part, mentally replay them, seeing yourself
succeed, and then "stepping into" your success
so that you actively feel what you did to achieve
it. Go further than marking minor details; mark
big victories with memorable celebrations, with
souvenirs of your triumphs, or in an achievement
diary. Then summarize the feeling of success in
affirmations that you repeat to yourself regularly,
particularly when you need a confidence boost.

EXTENDING YOUR CONFIDENCE RANGE

Develop an image of yourself as someone who succeeds, even if that means you have to overcome challenges. Constantly stretch yourself; aim within your achievable range so that you can succeed, but also regularly do that little bit more than is comfortable. That way, you are always building your sense of inner competence and achievement. Keep extending the range of things you attempt in life; broadening your experience helps you develop the confidence that you can cope with anything.

FOCUS POINT

● Make your victories memorable by sharing them with friends. This will set you on the path to further successes.

▼ **Looking confident**
Inner confidence results in a relaxed and focused physiological state. It also works the other way round: if body language is confident, the mind will follow suit.

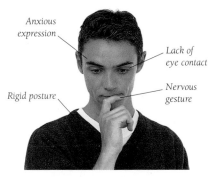

Anxious expression

Lack of eye contact

Rigid posture

Nervous gesture

Insecure body language

Open expression

Full eye contact

Relaxed posture

Level shoulders

Confident body language

Things to Do

✓ Do identify the most confident person you know. Ask them about how they remember successes and forget failures.

✓ Do look back over your achievement diary regularly, to remind yourself of how well you have done.

✓ Do practise confident body language, so that when you feel nervous, you can step into a confident mood.

Things to Avoid

✗ Avoid people who sap your confidence by diminishing your successes.

✗ Avoid unconfident thoughts; replace them by confidence-boosting affirmations, and repeat until you feel more relaxed.

✗ Avoid nervous paralysis when you need to be confident. Take a deep breath and stretch to release tension.

Setting Goals

Once you set a goal in life, the brain responds with a burst of activity that is experienced as happiness. When the goal is achieved, another burst of activity makes you happy again. To maintain a positive attitude, keep setting – and achieving – your goals.

SETTING THE GOAL

Whatever you are aiming for – a new job, a better level of fitness, or just a well-cooked meal – you need an achievable goal. Check first that you are clear about what you are aiming for; that it is something you really want; and that the time, energy, and resources required are worth the effort. Check also that when you reach your goal, what you gain will outweigh what you might lose. Your goal also needs to reflect your deeper values; if you do not believe in the worth of what you are doing, you will lack the energy to succeed.

▲ **Being motivated**
Having an aim, such as cooking a delicious meal for a friend, motivates you to excel, and this gives satisfaction.

Setting Goals

Set appropriate goal

⬇

Decide on incentives

⬇

Work out steps along the way

⬇

Take the first step

DEFINING THE STEPS

Before starting any task, break it down into its different stages. This will allow you to see the next step clearly and so have energy available for it, rather than viewing the task as a huge and endless effort. If you have performed the task before, revise what each step entails so that you know you are fully resourced to do it. If you have never done it before, talk to someone who has already succeeded. Then get going, whether you feel like it or not. You may think that effective people feel motivated to start things. But typically they do not; they start, and let their motivation build from the success of having begun.

Overcoming Demotivation

Demotivating Factor	Motivating Thought	Action
Fear of failure – you stop rather than risk failing	Failure is not the end of the world.	Make plans in case you do not succeed.
Comparison – you feel others would do better	Even successful people hit difficulties.	Regard others as mentors, not as competitors.
Reluctance – you never wanted to do it	I have the right to choose whether to do this.	Say no, or say yes and follow through.
Perfectionism – you have to do things excellently	My standards are impossibly high.	Lower standards and work up to success.
Lack of rewards – you never treat yourself	Without rewards, my body and mind will rebel.	Reward yourself for even the smallest success.
Lack of appreciation – no one says well done	People may not realize I need a pat on the back.	Actively ask others for positive feedback.

Treats herself to flowers

▲ **Rewarding yourself**
Keep motivated by setting yourself one small target at a time, and reward yourself each time you succeed.

MAINTAINING A MOTIVATED ATTITUDE

To keep your energy high, focus on incentives rather than penalties. You need to remind yourself of what you will lose if you fail, but it is more important to look forward to the rewards of success. And if those rewards do not yet feel very real and compelling, boost them until they are irresistible. Then, once you have embarked on a task, congratulate yourself for each small step you achieve – treat yourself to a new book, a new CD, a box of chocolates. The lower your level of motivation, the shorter the gaps between rewards should be. If the task is one you will repeat, keep a progress log. That way you can motivate yourself next time by looking back on your previous success.

Uncovering Meaning in Life

*T*he stronger a person's sense of purpose and meaning in life, the happier and more positive they will be. So, make a determined effort to find meaning in what you are doing, and cultivate beliefs and experiences that reflect that meaning.

66 Dreams are necessary to life. **99**

Anaïs Nin

▼ **Having a philosophy of life**
Knowing you have a purpose in life makes you more content day-to-day, as well as more able to face problems and crises with equanimity.

FINDING A FAITH
To have a happy life, you need a sense of an underlying point to your existence and of a moral code by which to live. This does not mean you have to have a religious or spiritual faith. It means you will feel more secure in yourself if you can sense a plan or a guiding force in life, and more at peace with the world if you have a workable set of principles. Take a few minutes each day to think about the values you wish to guide you, and try to cultivate beliefs and experiences that reflect them.

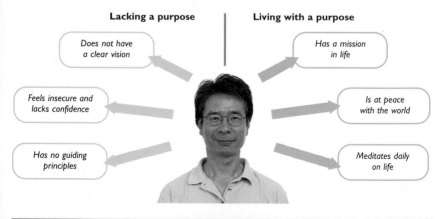

Lacking a purpose

Does not have a clear vision

Feels insecure and lacks confidence

Has no guiding principles

Living with a purpose

Has a mission in life

Is at peace with the world

Meditates daily on life

ACKNOWLEDGING YOUR MISSION

To live with a sense of purpose, you need to discover and keep in mind an ultimate mission in the world. If you do not yet have a mission, imagine yourself at the end of a long and happy life, where you have achieved what you were born to achieve. Spot the theme that runs through your achievements – perhaps "loving", "being a good parent", "improving the world". This theme is your mission. Then track what you imagine having done during your life in order to achieve a complete life. These are the practical actions you will need to take in order to fulfil your mission.

▲ **Living life to the full**
Your mission in life might be to build a strong relationship with your children. Imagine yourself in years to come, looking back on your life, and see what you could do now to achieve your goal.

Fact File

The concept of "flow activity" was developed by Mihaly Csikszentmihalyi at the University of Chicago in the USA. His work culminated in a book published in 1991. He identified the emotional state that you enter when you focus on an activity wholeheartedly, entirely forgetting yourself and the here-and-now. To be truly content you need a regular dose of "flow" – at least three hours a week spent in non-work activities that stimulate and interest you.

GAINING A SENSE OF FLOW

Look over your life and ask yourself whether you are partaking regularly in a variety of activities that absorb you so deeply that you forget all your problems and concerns. Make sure you have a range of different work tasks and hobbies to engage and excite you. Actively seek out things to do that are creative and challenging, that calm the mind and create a contented mood – flow activities. A study made in the year 2000 by the MIND mental health charity suggests the following flow activities, listed in order of effectiveness: listening to music, gardening, writing, painting and drawing, drama, writing and reading poetry, crafts, walking, needlework or knitting, dancing.

Living a Positive Life

You get most from positive thinking if you apply it regularly and consistently across your life. So create an environment, a routine, and a lifestyle that constantly enhances your mood.

Creating a Positive Environment

Positivity is generated from inside you, but what happens outside matters too. Environmental factors can influence the way you feel. By creating a space where you can be relaxed, comfortable, and focused, you can improve your outlook.

CONSTRUCTING A RETREAT

It is vital for your wellbeing to have a place, however tiny, to which you can retreat that is created entirely to your taste. At home, your oasis of calm could be a corner of a room, a converted loft, or a garden shed. At work, it might be at your desk. Even if you have to share living or work space with others, make sure there is some aspect of it that makes you feel happy. If possible, choose your own furniture, pictures, and colours.

▲ Making "me time"
It is good to withdraw from your hectic world regularly. Set aside some time to read or to meditate on a calming topic.

PROVIDING COMFORT

When you create your perfect space, indulge all your senses. Do not feel you "should" plan your decor according to fashion; instead, choose only what seems beautiful to you. Introduce plenty of natural light. At home, have a comfortable sofa or big cushions; at work, put flowers on your desk. Use scents to energize or relax you. You may want to play music to raise your mood, or you may prefer the background sound of water or wind chimes.

" To do nothing is sometimes a good remedy. "

Hippocrates

FINDING A MENTAL RETREAT

However supportive your environment, it is good to withdraw from it regularly, and retreat inside your head. Set aside a few minutes every day when you turn off the phone and relax. Still your mind, perhaps by concentrating on your breathing, or by focusing on a lit candle or a flower. Then you may choose to say a positive affirmation to yourself, or think through some significant topic. As your "me time" ends, take a few moments to recover, and return to the world.

COLOUR THEORY

When deciding the decor of your room, remember that colour affects mood. Build positivity by combining mood-lifting shades (avoid black, brown, and grey):

- Blue: calms, settles
- Yellow: invigorates, warms
- Green: soothes, harmonizes
- Red: stimulates, arouses
- Purple: energizes, inspires
- Orange: welcomes, warms
- White: enhances natural light

▲ **Creating a mood**
Select colours according to the atmosphere you want to create, whether it be gentle and tranquil, or stimulating and inspiring.

Improving Your Environment

Problem	Effect	Action to Take
High noise factor	Can distract, irritate, and frustrate.	Soundproof with rugs and curtains, or use headphones.
Low oxygen levels	Can create lethargy and low mood.	Open windows, install plants and a humidifier.
Lack of organization	Can confuse and make you feel out of control.	Buy storage systems and throw away clutter.

Building Health for Positivity

It is widely accepted that there is a link between physical health and mental well-being. To maintain a positive way of living, you need to support your mental approach with the right diet, exercise, and stress-reduction programme.

Shops regularly for fresh foods

Buys plenty of fruit and vegetables

▲ **Enjoying the good life**
A varied and well-balanced diet plays a significant role in maintaining balanced emotions.

EATING FOR POSITIVITY

You are what you eat. And there is increasing evidence that poor diet can send your body into a downward spiral of negative emotions. If you eat foods that make your blood-sugar level soar, that produce an adrenalin rush, or that trigger food intolerance, you are likely to spend your days on a rollercoaster of emotion. Choose a diet that avoids refined carbohydrates and refined sugars, and where possible eat unprocessed foods with no additives in order to avoid bad reactions to artificial colourings and flavourings.

FOCUS POINTS

● If you need to lose weight, follow a balanced diet and exercise more, rather than eating less.

● Avoid eating too many of the key foods that may trigger intolerance, such as wheat and dairy products.

CHOOSING THE BEST DIET

Your brain naturally produces certain neuro-transmitters one of whose functions is to help you feel good. In particular, serotonin keeps you calm, focused, and optimistic, while dopamine and norepinephrine keep you alert and active. Choose a diet that is designed to support their long-term production: for seratonin, eat foods rich in unrefined carbohydrate, such as cereals, pasta, rice, and starchy vegetables; for dopamine and norepinephrine, eat foods rich in amino acids, such as chicken, fish, beef, nuts, and pulses.

Foods with a Feelgood Factor

Nutrient	Source
B vitamins	Lean meat, fish, wholegrains, nuts, orange juice, low-fat dairy food, yeast extract, and pulses
Calcium	Milk, cheese, tinned fish, green leafy vegetables, nuts, and seeds
Folic acid	Green vegetables, wheatgerm, oranges, cheese, nuts, eggs, and liver
Iron	Wheatbran, liver, spinach, and dried fruit
Magnesium	Nuts, fish, leafy green vegetables, and wheatgerm
Omega 3 fats	Oily fish (mackerel, salmon, sardines, trout) and vegetable oils (grapeseed, soya, sunflower)
Selenium	Brazil nuts, shellfish, liver, fish, and wholegrains

▼ **Eating well**
Low mood has been linked with deficiencies of some vitamins and minerals. Follow a diet that includes oily fish such as salmon, lean meat, green vegetables, and pulses.

ESTABLISHING A GOOD REGIME

There is sense in the old adage: breakfast like a king, dine like a pauper. Eating breakfast gives you a feelgood start to the day by kickstarting your body with much-needed fuel after its overnight starvation. Conversely, eating a light meal in the evening means your body does not have to cope with the strain of digesting food, and you will fall asleep more easily.

In between times, avoid "comfort" foods and drinks such as chocolate and caffeine. While they may give you an instant lift, their feelgood effect may suddenly dip, leaving you feeling even more down than before. Regular low-sugar snacks will keep your energy level – and your mood – high.

49

TAKING EXERCISE

If you want to raise your mood, keep moving. Exercise builds health – and a healthy body is conducive to a happy mind. Exercise helps counteract stress, and increases the production of feelgood brain chemicals. Create an exercise regime that you enjoy and can maintain – 20 minutes three times a week is a good basic minimum. It should leave you feeling relaxed and good about yourself.

Releasing Tension

> **Take a deep breath and let it out**

⬇

> **Yawn to relax yourself and get more oxygen into the bloodstream**

⬇

> **Consciously slow down what you are doing**

⬇

> **Think of the positive side of what is happening**

⬇

> **Repeat a relaxing affirmation, such as "I am calm"**

▲ **Exercising for a healthy mind**
Choose a form of exercise that you like – and do not overdo it. If you are competitive, play team games. If you like company, find a gym buddy. If you love the outdoors, go running.

SLEEPING SOUNDLY

If you are not sleeping properly, you will have difficulty in thinking positively; lack of sleep creates mental confusion, stress, and depression. Experiment to find the right amount of sleep for you. If you have difficulty in sleeping, this is most likely to be due to stress during your day, or a lack of preparation for sleep. Avoid evening activities that leave you overstimulated, such as watching scary movies or listening to loud music. Instead, set up a relaxed pre-bed routine, doing the same things, at the same time. Stick to the same waking and sleeping hours, if possible.

Assessing Your Stress Levels

How stressed do you feel in your life at the moment? Tick any of the following statements that describe you accurately:

- I find it hard to switch off when I go to bed. ☐

- I often get upset or angry about what happens to me. ☐

- I suffer from stress-related sickness, such as headaches. ☐

- I do not get much joy out of work or play. ☐

- I feel I am not coping with life at the moment. ☐

Analysis The higher the number of ticks, the more stressed you are. Take action to reduce the stress in your life so that you are better able to cope with it.

BALANCING STRESS LEVELS

You will find it difficult to be positive when you are under stress, not only because your body and mind are on alert, looking for problems, but also because you are likely to feel fragile. Be aware of stress – at work, in relationships, or from family matters – and take immediate action to reduce it. Say no to unrealistic demands. Try to sort out the problems in your life. Take time – a daily half-hour, a weekly half-day – to do off-task things and unwind. Be aware when stress comes from being underused or bored, and make sure you are stretching yourself just the right amount in your life. Get support: talk through problems with someone who can listen and support you.

Lies comfortably, with plenty of head support

Tenses each part of body in turn, then relaxes

Relaxing effectively ▶
Relaxing for 15 minutes a day can have a cumulative effect on reducing stress in your life and so make you feel more positive. Make relaxation exercises part of your daily routine.

❝ Take rest: a field that has rested gives a bountiful crop. **❞**

Ovid

Useful Exercises

▶ Work out a plan for regular exercise and write it into your diary or stick it on your pinboard.

▶ In bed, write down anything bothering you, so your mind knows it need not worry overnight.

▶ Before you go to sleep, repeat a calming affirmation, such as, "I shall sleep until morning".

Forming Good Relationships

Positive thinking means being positive with other people as well as with yourself. Dealing well with others creates good relationships, and the more good relationships you have in your life, the more emotionally resilient you are likely to be.

GIVING PRAISE

All successful relationships are based on mutual respect. So open up and tell others if they impress you. They will appreciate it more if you give them details about what you like and if you express your feelings as well as just your thoughts. Beware of qualification – do not praise a good performance, only to compare it with an earlier failure. And remember that regular, dripfed appreciation is much better than a deluge followed by a drought.

◄ Building confidence
Giving your children encouragement and praise will focus their attention on success and build confidence for the future.

Things to Do	Things to Avoid
✓ Do make a habit of showing praise and appreciation regularly.	✗ Avoid praising all the time. People may think they have done something wrong if the praise suddenly stops.
✓ Do offer praise "sandwiches" – two pieces of positive feedback enclosing a suggestion or request for improvement.	✗ Avoid praising things for courtesy's sake; such false compliments devalue genuine praise.
✓ Do follow through your congratulatory words with positive body language – a smile, nod, or touch where appropriate.	✗ Avoid praising success only. This gives the message that effort is worthless.

Keeps eye contact

Feels valued

Leans forward to show interest

▲ **Using positive body language**
Approving body language is the most direct way that you can tell someone you feel positive about them and get them to feel good about themselves and respond well to you.

ADOPTING A NO-BLAME ATTITUDE

Even if you feel bad about what someone does, avoid heavy criticism. Work off any critical emotion by writing your feelings out in a letter that you never send or by imagining a conversation. If you still feel you need to give the person feedback, begin by pointing out what they have done right, to help them feel confident. Then, specify what you need them to do, in positives rather than negatives. Lastly, look for improvement in behaviour and reinforce it by praising as soon as you can.

COPING WITH CRITICISM

If someone criticizes you, stay calm. Let your critic say their piece so that they feel they are being heard. But take on board only what feels right; offset any hurt by recalling times you have done well. If you sense the criticism is correct, particularly if you have had similar feedback from others, ask your critic to coach you in improving. This will not only mean you are supported to learn; it will also get him or her on your side, building a relationship out of a potentially tense interaction.

FINDING REASON TO FORGIVE

When something has gone wrong and you cannot immediately find forgiveness – for yourself or another person – look back carefully at what has happened, and you may see the situation in a different light. Perhaps there were valid reasons why you or the other person did what they did, or maybe it was a difficult time or situation. It could be that what happened actually caused no harm, or that it is outweighed by good things you or the other person have done. Perhaps that was the only or best choice of action under the circumstances at the time.

A token of forgiveness
If you find you can forgive the other person, you may like to show it with a small gift.

CHOOSING THE RIGHT PEOPLE

Actively avoid negative people, who drain your energy, bore you, always see the worst side of life, or bring you down. If possible, simply stop seeing them; go through your address book and remove their names. If you have to spend time with them, reduce the amount of contact and spend your freed-up time with people who leave you feeling good about yourself and the world. Expand your range of supportive friends; if you meet someone who seems content with themselves and their life, actively suggest you spend time together.

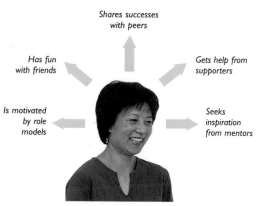

Shares successes with peers

Has fun with friends

Gets help from supporters

Is motivated by role models

Seeks inspiration from mentors

Self-Talk

If, despite your efforts, you find yourself continuing to mix with overdemanding or unhelpful people, you are probably suffering from a belief that you deserve no better. Use affirmations such as those given below to rethink this belief as a more positive one. Repeat them to yourself regularly.

❝I deserve to be surrounded with people who value and respect me.❞

❝It is fine for me to take from as well as give to people.❞

❝The more positive people I mix with, the more able I will be to pass that positivity on.❞

◀ **Enjoying good company**
Make sure you surround yourself with different types of positive people – people who, in one way or another, boost rather than drain your energy.

FOCUS POINTS

● Build a network of mentors for guidance on a variety of life skills.

● If you feel a problem is sliding out of control, consider seeking help from a counsellor.

NETWORKING

To get positive people around you, actively network. Friends and supporters do not appear by magic, and you may have to meet many people before you bond with someone. Regularly go to networking events, professional and personal. Remember that others may be shy, and will be grateful if you make the first move. Exchange contact details. Next day, phone or e-mail saying how good it was to meet; then a few weeks later follow up with a date and time to meet again.

Showing you care
Sending postcards while you are on holiday is a quick and easy way of keeping in touch with friends.

KEEPING IN TOUCH

Actively nurture established and new relationships by making contact on a regular basis. Write postcards to friends and family when you are on holiday, send cards for religious festivals, and remember birthdays and wedding anniversaries with cards or flowers. Write reminders into your diary so that too much time does not lapse between meetings. If you are pushed for time, create group events – parties, picnics, theatre trips – to which you can invite a number of your friends at one time.

ENROLLING HELP

Most people are very happy to help if asked; it makes them feel needed and therefore valued. But they will give support much more readily if it is part of a regular, reciprocal arrangement. So make a list of people in your life whose skills and talents you really value. This will be your support system. The next time you meet one of those people, ask for help in some small way, offering a similar favour in return. Maintain this give-and-take, so that if you ever need more substantial help, it will be much easier to ask.

❝ You can discover more about a person in an hour of play than in a year of conversation. ❞

Plato

▲ **Mixing with kindred spirits**
Good relationships are about mutual support. A party is the ideal opportunity to cultivate friendships with those who share a positive outlook on life and will be there for you when you need help.

Loving with Heart

If you want to be loved, be positive. Positive people are fun to be with, confident in their own abilities, able to give and take. The end result of their positive outlook is that they find, develop, and maintain relationships easily.

BEING PROUD OF YOURSELF

To gain love, begin with a strong, positive image of yourself. The more you believe you are attractive, the more others will believe it too. Remember that while appearance is important, most people do not need a partner who is perfectly good-looking or has a stunning figure; confidence and personality are very much more compelling. Be proud of your appearance and your character – and above all, believe you deserve love.

66 The best way to cheer yourself up is to try to cheer someone else up. 99

Mark Twain

WELCOMING A POTENTIAL PARTNER

Being genuinely positive about other people is immensely seductive. If you like someone, let it show. Pose questions, then listen carefully to the answers. Make it clear you are interested. Talk – without taking over the conversation – about your own thoughts and feelings, to show you trust the other person. Once you have established that there is some rapport, do not hold back. Instead, be upfront about wanting to meet again.

Touches lightly to show willingness to become more intimate

Nods and smiles to show approval

Stands close

▲ **Displaying interest**
By showing you feel positive about a potential partner non-verbally as well as verbally, you signal your attraction at both the conscious and the unconscious level.

MAKING LOVE WORK

Once your relationship is under way, be optimistic. Particularly if past relationships have gone wrong, you may be wary and guarded, constantly looking for problems. However, this approach is guaranteed to lay the foundations for a fraught, sad partnership. Instead, think the best of your partner; not only will you bring out the best in them, you will also help them to feel good about themselves. And be optimistic about your love relationship; you will create the energy needed to make it a happy one. Put the emphasis on enjoyment, having fun together, and making each other feel good.

▼ Holding on to joy
Putting aside regular time for having some fun together is one of the keys to a successful relationship. Aim to have five positive interactions for each negative one.

Assessing Your Relationship

Negative interaction	Key questions	Positive interaction
You never bother to ask how the day went	**Do you keep lines of communication open?**	You show an interest in each other's day
You ignore the situation or express criticism	**Do you support your partner when he or she has problems?**	You show sympathy even if you feel critical
You have no one-to-one time, no shared interests	**Do you regularly take time for yourselves as a couple?**	You put aside one evening a week, one day a month

OVERCOMING DIFFERENCES

You and your partner have different outlooks and different personalities. That is refreshing when you first meet, but sometimes you grow to resent these differences. Instead, put energy into understanding why your partner thinks and feels as they do. Ask them to explain their point of view. Explore how their attitudes have been formed, and appreciate their views, even if you cannot agree. Your partner will then feel more able to understand you and your outlook. Think the best of your partner and you will bring out the best in him or her.

At a Glance

● Having the energy to love your partner is only possible if you love yourself.

● Being positive about your partner brings out the best.

● In a partnership, loving is a better strategy than winning.

● A successful couple is not one where partners never differ. It is one where they capitalize on their differences.

FOCUS POINTS

● If your relationship is giving more pain than pleasure, seek counselling.

● If your relationship comes to an end, move on without regret.

RESOLVING DISAGREEMENTS

Most couples disagree with each other sometimes, however content they are; the happiest couples are those that learn to manage those disagreements and find "win–win" solutions wherever possible. The key is to maintain a good mood; stay calm yourself, and help your partner to stay calm too by reassuring him or her that you still care. Negotiate to resolve the conflict. Find places where your needs overlap, and reach a compromise.

◀ **Resolving conflict**
Managing disagreement is a question of give-and-take. Experiment with solutions to meet both your needs. Check that both of you are happy with the agreement you reach, to ensure you carry it through.

SOOTHING BAD FEELING

When simple disagreement turns to active conflict, both you and your partner may feel angry. In fact, you are both afraid – that the other will disappoint, reject, control, or walk away. Understand this, and you will feel less threatened, less defensive, and more open. When things become heated, rather than nagging or shouting, say what it is that you are afraid will happen. Rather than blaming or attacking, ask what it is that frightens your partner. Expressing fears helps you to sympathize, rather than attack.

Partners come to a decision that suits them both, and the relationship is enriched

▼ **Dealing with conflict**
A positive approach to conflict between a couple involves communication, co-operation, and shared decision-making.

Partners listen to each other; she researches costs, he looks for alternative cars

He fails to ask her point of view. She does not share her fear that they cannot afford the car

Couple disagrees about spending money on a new car

He buys a car anyway. She feels angry, he feels guilty, and the relationship becomes strained

Things to Do	Things to Avoid
✔ Do celebrate – even the most defensive person feels calmed when told they are appreciated and valued.	✗ Avoid sniping or nagging – neither of these gets results and both increase antagonism between you.
✔ Do offer physical contact – a hugged partner is a less-threatened partner.	✗ Avoid bringing up the past – instead focus on the problem that you are faced with here and now.
✔ Do try to defuse tension – a smile or a joke can turn a looming argument into a friendly discussion.	✗ Avoid letting conflict drag on – find a solution, then kiss and make up.

Working with Energy

M ost people spend a third of their adult lives at work. So it is vital to make sure that when you are working, you feel positive about what you do. In that way your career supports rather than undermines your positive approach to life.

MOTIVATING YOURSELF AT WORK

The essence of a happy job is to work with what is important to you, the things in life that really attract you. If you like people, work with them. If you love knowledge or ideas, or clothes, or words, find work that involves these. Be sure to chart your successes. Identify how you can do well, and then get regular feedback on how to do even better. And keep moving on: if you are stuck at your current level, learn how to do your current job even better than you already do it, so that you still experience improvement.

▼ **Making the best of things**
The positive thinker who is unhappy at work takes action to improve things. If you feel negative about your job, try to become more rather than less involved. The more you actively contribute, the more control you will have.

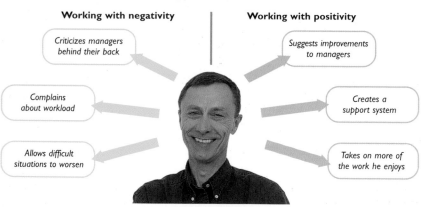

Working with negativity

Criticizes managers behind their back

Complains about workload

Allows difficult situations to worsen

Working with positivity

Suggests improvements to managers

Creates a support system

Takes on more of the work he enjoys

CREATING POSITIVE RELATIONSHIPS

Being pleasant to colleagues and clients creates a good working relationship, even when you are in competition or opposed. Speak well of others. Congratulate their successes, even when you lose out. Take responsibility for your errors rather than shifting the blame; never crow over your victories if they mean defeat for others. Be a positive force, celebrating when things go well, and offering solutions and support when things go badly.

▲ **Interacting positively**
Colleagues and clients alike respond positively to an enthusiastic attitude. With her open and friendly manner, this manager is likely to motivate colleagues to perform well.

Assessing Your Job Satisfaction

How positive do you feel about your work? Tick any statements that you think describe you accurately:

● I typically look forward to work in the morning. ☐

● I feel my job is meaningful and fulfilling. ☐

● I have as much energy and enthusiasm for work as I have ever had. ☐

● I feel appreciated by colleagues and clients. ☐

● I only occasionally feel angry or upset at work. ☐

● I ignore job ads because moving is not on my mind. ☐

Analysis The fewer ticks you have, the more unhappy you are. Look at these items again and plan how you can make work a positive experience.

STAYING POSITIVE

Paid work is rarely fun all the time, but having a constructive attitude will help to keep the mood high. Come to work with a smile and keep smiling, even under pressure. Be enthusiastic rather than critical when you discuss your employers or your work. If you are unhappy, talk to the management assertively, to suggest improvements.

Coping Day to Day

When one tiny problem makes you feel negative, you can all too easily find yourself creating more problems for yourself, and the day turns into a disaster. The answer is to act immediately to stop the downward spiral. Then you can begin to cope again.

FEELING A SENSE OF ACHIEVEMENT

Sometimes when something small goes wrong it can trigger a domino effect, where each problem leads to a bigger one. The solution is to take action to inject immediate positivity into the situation and avert a crisis. Do something that gives you a sense of success. Choose a small, specific task that you have done many times before and that you know you are not going to fail at. Choose something that has instant rewards, a visible result, or positive feedback. Do something that you have been avoiding, to give you even more of a sense of victory. So send that e-mail, sew on that button, water that plant. The sense of achievement you feel when you have done it will turn the tide.

FOCUS POINTS

● To prevent a problem becoming a crisis, ensure the basic human needs of success, esteem, and control are all being met.

● If you are dragged down by feelings of panic, take a short break to renew objectivity and get things in perspective.

Feeling good ▶

If you feel unable to cope, set yourself a simple task you know you will be able to complete easily – perhaps a small job in the garden. Then build on the sense of achievement you get from completing it.

REALIZING YOUR VALIDITY

A day where nothing goes right can quickly lower your self-esteem and make you feel worthless. Do something that gives you an instant boost in validity. Avoid self-indulgences that have a backlash, such as alcohol, bingeing on sugary food, or overspending. Instead, give yourself a totally positive treat, to prove you are worth it – a walk in the park, a good book to read, a massage. Contact someone who cares about you, tell them how you feel, and ask them to list your good points. Find someone who likes you, chat to them, and notice how they light up in response.

Fact File

A bad day can be even worse in winter. Up to six in every 100 people suffer from a type of winter depression known as Seasonal Affective Disorder (SAD). This is triggered by a biochemical imbalance in the brain, caused by lack of sunlight in the dark winter months. People prone to negativity in the winter should try to get as much natural daylight as possible through outside activities.

Useful Exercises

▶ If you are feeling tense, breathe in through your nose and lift your arms – then exhale forcefully while dropping your arms.

▶ Sniff eucalyptus, pine, mandarin, or basil essential oils for a calming effect.

▶ For a quick boost to your physical energy, walk around the room or jog on the spot for a few minutes.

REGAINING A SENSE OF CONTROL

As problem piles on problem, you may feel that you are losing control. You can get back on top, even in the smallest way, by imposing order and method over some aspect of what is happening. Tidy your desk, your bag, your computer files. Make a list of tasks and prioritize them. Plan in detail what you need to do for the rest of the day. Initiate a meeting or pick up the phone. As soon as you start to feel in control, you will begin to get back on track.

Creates a system for keeping papers organized

Files household accounts

▲ **Getting back on track**
When you are feeling stressed and overwhelmed, focus on resolving one small thing, for example, sorting your papers, and you will quickly begin to feel you are back in charge of your life.

Managing Life Events

Learning to handle life events – either coping with a sudden crisis or moving through a natural phase – will drain your positivity. Learn how to manage and benefit from these events, instead of finding that you are dragged down by them.

Case Study

NAME: Tom
ISSUE: Coping with divorce
OBJECTIVE: To re-engage with life

Tom's divorce has come as a shock. He feels sad about what he sees as a wasted relationship, and anxious about the future. Tom's family rallies round, and it helps that he and his wife have negotiated access to the children. In the first year after the divorce he has a few tentative dates, but then starts joining local organizations, including a singles group. By talking to others there, he starts to realize that there are opportunities after divorce. Eighteen months later he is dating seriously, he has bought a flat, and he is decorating it.

HANDLING CRISES

A life crisis, such as illness, redundancy, loss of trust, divorce, or death, can leave you feeling helpless and depressed for a long time. Aim to cope stage by stage. Take immediate action to sort the practical issues and regain a sense of control. Once the first shock is over, think – or better, talk – through what has happened to get things in perspective. Later, focus on what you have learned from the crisis. Remember that a crisis is almost always temporary; in time the pain will fade away.

▲ **Facing bad news**
A breaking crisis such as illness or bereavement can trigger reactions of disbelief, denial, shock. Take time to get support from those around you before facing facts and taking action to cope.

Facing Life Events with Positivity

Life Stage	Sadness About	Worry About	The Up Side
Committing to a relationship	Giving up independence.	Whether love will survive.	Security and love given and received.
Starting a family	Sacrificing day-to-day freedom.	Burden of responsibility.	The joy of seeing your child grow.
Hitting career plateau	Passing the peak of achievement.	Going downhill.	Being free of work pressures.
Seeing children leave home	Ending active role as parent.	Future loneliness.	Being free of responsibility.
Retiring	Losing work role.	Having nothing to do.	More free "me time".
Reaching old age	Unfulfilled ambitions.	Future mortality.	Increased ability to be at ease with self.

MANAGING CHANGE

Life contains natural stages, such as marriage, parenthood, and retirement, where you move from one life role to another. Look ahead and prepare for change. Talk to others who have been through that phase about how to survive the challenges, and how to reap the rewards ahead. Once you have moved into a new stage, be prepared for shifts in your approach to life. Update those close to you on these changes, so they avoid confusion and frustration, and can adapt to your new attitude to life.

Acknowledges change in role now son is ready for adult life

Looking to the future ▶
Parent and child need to prepare for the emotions heralded by the end of full-time education. To navigate any change in life role, give yourself time to let go of the old and prepare for the new.

Ageing with Attitude

Positive thinking can alter the length as well as the quality of life. It is generally accepted that with a positive outlook on life not only can you move into the later years feeling both fulfilled and contented, you can also actively prolong your life.

Cheerful expression

Smart appearance

Upright posture

Brisk movement

◄ **Looking good**
Taking care of your appearance not only makes you feel better, but also gives the message that age has in no way reduced your capabilities

REALIZING THE BENEFITS

The key to ageing positively is to realize that, with current health care and society's support, ageing is now a positive experience. You can stay fit, healthy, and active until well into your eighth and ninth decade. Your increased knowledge will easily offset the very small decrease in mental capacity. Your gathered life-wisdom means that you can emotionally outperform younger generations. And with added experience, there is no reason why your capacity for sexual pleasure should not keep increasing with every passing year.

Self-Talk

Switch any typically "older" attitudes to the attitudes that younger people have, and you will see your life become more enjoyable and positive. Try telling yourself:

❝ I love doing… ❞

❝ Young people inspire me… ❞

❝ It will be an adventure… ❞

❝ At my age, I can… ❞

ACTING ENERGETICALLY

Ageing often makes you likely to settle for the comfortable option, the familiar idea. But every time you do that, you block off future fulfillment by being less willing to take risks or experiment. The key is to expand your comfort zone, do things that at first you do not find easy. Expose yourself to extremes: listen to loud music, watch films outside your normal range, eat an exotic meal. Seek out challenging activities: get up to dance, volunteer for extra responsibility. It may feel hard. But if you go for it, you will start to enjoy a wider range of life experiences.

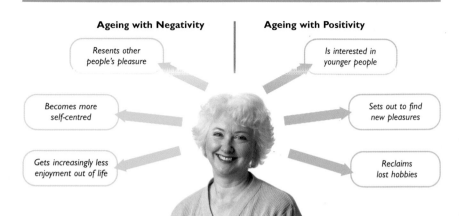

Ageing with Negativity

Resents other people's pleasure

Becomes more self-centred

Gets increasingly less enjoyment out of life

Ageing with Positivity

Is interested in younger people

Sets out to find new pleasures

Reclaims lost hobbies

▲ **Staying young at heart**
As you get older you may find you start to resent the youthfulness of others. If your capacity for pleasure is declining, make a point of looking out for people who enjoy themselves, and learn to have fun with them.

REMAINING FLEXIBLE

Once you reach the age of 30, your thinking may start to get more rigid and pessimistic. You will probably not realize this is happening; you may even find rational explanations for being more wary, cautious, and dogmatic! But mental flexibility is vital to positivity. So keep your brain active. Do puzzles. Have challenging conversations. If you disagree with someone, try to see their side of the argument and leave it at that. If you feel judgemental, imagine being in their position. If you feel strongly critical about something, think back to a time when you felt more tolerant about it, and reclaim that point of view.

Keeping alert ▶
Reading keeps you interested and interesting, and is an excellent way of keeping your mind active.

FOCUS POINT

● Remember that the beauty that comes from an appealing personality grows year on year.

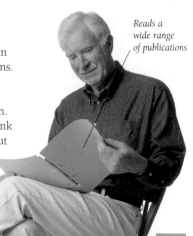

Reads a wide range of publications

How Positive Are You Now?

N*ow spend some time putting into practice what you have learned. Then look at the following statements and mark the answers closest to your experience. Be as honest as you can: if your answer is "Never", mark Option 1; if it is "Always", mark Option 4; and so on. Add your scores together, then refer to the analysis.*

Options	
1	Never
2	Occasionally
3	Frequently
4	Always

How Do You Respond?

	1	2	3	4
1 I love having a positive approach to life.	☐	☐	☐	☐
2 I feel good about other people.	☐	☐	☐	☐
3 I am aware when I think negatively.	☐	☐	☐	☐
4 I challenge my negative thoughts.	☐	☐	☐	☐
5 I keep my internal pictures positive.	☐	☐	☐	☐
6 I always use positive language.	☐	☐	☐	☐
7 I actively build helpful beliefs.	☐	☐	☐	☐
8 I feel good about myself.	☐	☐	☐	☐
9 I bounce back if my positivity slips.	☐	☐	☐	☐

	1	2	3	4
10 I manage my painful emotions well.	☐	☐	☐	☐
11 I have no regrets about the past.	☐	☐	☐	☐
12 I steer clear of blame and self-blame.	☐	☐	☐	☐
13 I use assertiveness to meet my needs.	☐	☐	☐	☐
14 I can snap out of anxiety.	☐	☐	☐	☐
15 I am optimistic about life.	☐	☐	☐	☐
16 I frequently enjoy myself.	☐	☐	☐	☐
17 I have plenty of confidence.	☐	☐	☐	☐
18 I set goals, and achieve them.	☐	☐	☐	☐

	1	2	3	4
19 I have meaning in my life.	☐	☐	☐	☐
20 I have an environment that supports me.	☐	☐	☐	☐
21 I make time to de-stress.	☐	☐	☐	☐
22 I eat a balanced and healthy diet.	☐	☐	☐	☐
23 I take the exercise I need.	☐	☐	☐	☐
24 I have a satisfying social network.	☐	☐	☐	☐
25 I am comfortable asking for support.	☐	☐	☐	☐

	1	2	3	4
26 I both give and receive love.	☐	☐	☐	☐
27 I can resolve conflict in my partnership.	☐	☐	☐	☐
28 I use positive thinking in my workplace.	☐	☐	☐	☐
29 I can turn round a really bad day.	☐	☐	☐	☐
30 I expect life to change – and I cope!	☐	☐	☐	☐
31 I feel better about life the older I get.	☐	☐	☐	☐
32 I feel the world is a great place.	☐	☐	☐	☐

Analysis

When you have added up your scores, look at the analysis below. Note areas where you are doing well and areas where you still need to improve. Compare your scores with those on your initial assessment on pages 12–13 to see how far you have come.

96–128 Well done – your approach to life is very positive indeed. All you need to do is keep practising your skills.

65–95 You are positive, but there is still work to be done. Reread the relevant parts of the book to make improvements.

32–64 Positivity is still very hard for you. Keep practising the strategies in this book, and get outside support, such as counselling, to help you win through.

My weakest areas are:

_____

_____

_____

_____

My strongest areas are:

_____

_____

_____

_____

Index

Acknowledgments

AUTHOR'S ACKNOWLEDGMENTS

I would like to thank the following people who have helped me create this book: My office team of Michelle Woolley, Sarah Stannard, Linda Newman, Nicola Renson, and Colin Marsh; my agent, Barbara Levy; my colleagues and friends John Seymour and Martin Shervington, Carl Boston, and Simon Anscombe. A special thank you to Lyndel Costain BSc, SRD, Consultant Dietitian, for her support on the sections dealing with nutrition.

Thanks also to Stephanie Jackson, Adèle Hayward, Hazel Richardson, and Jacky Jackson at Dorling Kindersley, and Sue Gordon and Dawn Terrey at Studio Cactus for their much appreciated assistance. A final thank you to my husband Ian, who always makes even the impossible possible.

PUBLISHER'S ACKNOWLEDGMENTS

Dorling Kindersley would like to thank the following for their help and participation on the first edition:

Project Editor Nicky Munro; **Senior Art Editor** Sarah Cowley;
DTP Designer Rajen Shah; **Production Controller** Mandy Inness;
Managing Editor Adèle Hayward; **Managing Art Editor** Marianne Markham;
Category Publisher Stephanie Jackson

Design Assistant Dennis Buckley; **Editorial Assistant** Laura Seber;
Design Consultant Laura Watson; **Editorial Consultant** Kate Hayward;
Jacket Designer John Dinsdale; **Jacket Editor** Jane Oliver-Jedrzejak;
Indexer Hilary Bird; **Proofreader** John Sturges; **Photography** Steve Gorton

Models Angela Cameron, Cameron Moss, Claire Moore, Hannah Fuller, Jackie Jennings, Jan Davidson, John Sturges, Kathleen McMahon, Kit Trew, Kuo Kang Chen, Laura Seber, Marilyn Reynolds, Mei Lien Chen, Nick Sherlock, Philip Holloway, Tom Jennings; **Make-up** Carolyn Boult

Picture research by Ilumi; **Picture librarian** Lucy Claxton

The Author and Publishers are grateful to the Estate of Anaïs Nin for the use of the quotation on page 44.

PICTURE CREDITS
The publisher would like to thank the following for their kind permission to reproduce their photographs:

Key: *a*=above; *b*=bottom; *c*=centre; *l*=left; *r*=right; *t*=top
Corbis: Duomo 8; Jose Luis Pelaez Inc 27*c*, 61; David Raymer 42; Tom Stewart 46; Rick Gomez 52;
Getty Images: Jim Bastardo 4/5; Photodisc 18; Jacobs Stock Photography 22; D. Berry/Photodisc 25*b*;
Nick Dolding/Taxi 30, 57; Eyewire 36*b*, 62; Ryanstock/Taxi 40; Stockbyte 45; Tony Anderson 50;
Ryan McVay/Photodisc 55*b*; David Hanover/Stone 64*b*.

All other images © Dorling Kindersley
For further information see: www.dkimages.com